TEACHER PLANNER

— FOR THE —

SECONDARY CLASSROOM

A COMPANION TO

Discipline in the Secondary Classroom

BY RANDALL S. SPRICK, PH.D.

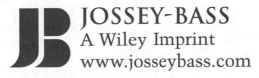

JOSSEY-BASS
A Wiley Imprint
www.josseybass.com

RANDY SPRICK'S

safe & civil
SCHOOLS

Practical Solutions, Positive Results!

JOSSEY-BASS TEACHER

Jossey-Bass Teacher provides educators with practical knowledge and tools to create a positive and lifelong impact on student learning. We offer classroom-tested and research-based teaching resources for a variety of grade levels and subject areas. Whether you are an aspiring, new, or veteran teacher, we want to help you make every teaching day your best.

From ready-to-use classroom activities to the latest teaching framework, our value-packed books provide insightful, practical, and comprehensive materials on the topics that matter most to K–12 teachers. We hope to become your trusted source for the best ideas from the most experienced and respected experts in the field.

TEACHER PLANNER
— FOR THE —
SECONDARY CLASSROOM

TEACHER PLANNER FOR THE
SECONDARY CLASSROOM

YEAR: _____

I've come to the frightening conclusion that I am the decisive element in the classroom. It's my personal approach that creates the climate. It's my daily mood that makes the weather.

As a teacher,
I possess a tremendous amount of power to make a child's life miserable or joyous.

I can be a tool of torture or an instrument of inspiration.

I can humiliate or humor, hurt or heal.

In all situations, it is my response that decides whether a crisis will be escalated or de-escalated and a child humanized or de-humanized.

—*Haim Ginott*

Name _____

E-mail _____

SCHOOL

School/Rm. _____

Address _____

City/State _____ Zip _____

Phone _____

HOME

Address _____

City/State _____ Zip _____

Phone _____

TABLE OF CONTENTS

references

If you have a copy of *Discipline in the Secondary Classroom* (2nd ed.), watch for the reference boxes throughout this planner.

USER'S GUIDE

The *TEACHER PLANNER FOR THE SECONDARY CLASSROOM* includes activities that will help you improve student responsibility and motivation throughout the school year. Planner activities can be used on their own, but are best used to preview and/or review the in-depth procedural knowledge learned from reading *DISCIPLINE IN THE SECONDARY CLASSROOM ("DSC")*.

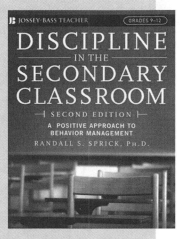

Note: A completed sample lesson plan can be found on p. 126. Reproducible forms that appear in this planner are also available as fillable PDFs on the *DSC* companion DVD.

Lesson Planners • Getting Started

1. Using your school calendar, enter dates for each week. Forty-two Weekly Planners are included.

2. Fill in holidays, vacations, teacher workdays, parent conferences, testing, field trips, assemblies, etc.

3. Set up a planner schedule. There are 35 writing lines on each weekly planner spread. Divide 35 lines by the number of periods and your lunch period. Use a pencil to draw lines across the planner to separate the periods. Repeat with a pencil or pen for subsequent weeks.

Getting the Year Started

1. Before school begins, read and complete the activities on pp. 4–17 of this planner.

2. Identify when you will complete a Grade Book Analysis (one week before the end of each quarter or trimester). Write a reminder in your planner to do the Grade Book Analysis.

Throughout the Year

Conduct *DSC* activities as they come up in your planner (or sooner). Repeat these activities as appropriate. See the Table of Contents for the sequence and frequency of planned *DSC* activities.

Watch for the weekly Planner Tip.

Teach with inspiration and enthusiasm!

Vision • Guidelines for Success

Guidelines for Success are a set of four or five noble goals that can help your students be successful in your classroom, throughout their school careers, and in the world of work.

> **Guidelines for Success**
> 1. Be responsible.
> 2. Do your best.
> 3. Cooperate with others.
> 4. Treat everyone with respect (including yourself).

- ✓ Post your school's guidelines. If your school does not have guidelines, design your own.
- ✓ Teach the guidelines at the beginning of the year.
- ✓ Refer to the guidelines frequently to help students strive for excellence.
- ✓ Provide descriptive feedback to students as they demonstrate the traits, attitudes, and behaviors reflected in your guidelines.

EXAMPLE OF DESCRIPTIVE FEEDBACK:
Shelley, your homework was complete and on time this week. This will be reflected in your grade. Nice job.

TO DO

List Guidelines for Success.

Write • Classroom Rules
DEVELOP AND DISPLAY CLASSROOM RULES

1. Develop (or plan to have your students help you develop) three to six specific classroom rules. These rules will provide the basis for acknowledging appropriate behavior and implementing consequences for misbehavior. Unlike the noble ideas expressed in your Guidelines for Success, classroom rules are observable.
   - ✓ Rules should be stated positively.
   - ✓ Rules should be specific and refer to observable behaviors.
   - ✓ Rules must be applicable throughout the day or class period.
   - ✓ Rules should be posted in a prominent, visible location.
2. Design lessons to teach the rules using positive and negative examples.

TO DO

Write three to six classroom rules.

....

....

....

....

....

3. Develop correction procedures. As appropriate, use proximity, gentle verbal reprimands, discussion, humor, family contact, and restitution. (See *DSC*, pp. 130–40.)

4. Provide positive, descriptive feedback. Frequently link student behavior to the Guidelines for Success.

CLASSROOM RULES

1. Come to class every day that you are not seriously ill.
2. Arrive on time with paper, pencil or pen, textbook, and notebook with a divider for science.
3. Keep your hands, feet, and objects to yourself.
4. Follow directions the first time they are given.
5. Stay on task during all work times.

sample

FAQ

What's the difference between classroom rules and Guidelines for Success?

An analogy may help: When driving, we have rules of the road, such as "Stop at a stop sign." Rules of the road are enforceable and analogous to classroom rules. On the other hand, a Guideline for Success might be "Be a courteous driver." The guideline is broader and less specific.

LESSON PLAN

Post the rules.

Explain the rules. Link the rules to your Guidelines for Success.

One of our Guidelines for Success is "Be responsible." You can demonstrate this by following the class rule "Follow directions the first time they are given." This is an important rule because it will be an expectation if you play sports and when you get a job. When you follow instructions or directions the first time they are given, our work progresses smoothly, efficiently, and pleasantly.

Demonstrate and/or have students role-play each rule. Use positive and negative examples, with feedback and discussion after each example.

Ask: Was that following directions the first time they were given? Why or why not?

Direction: Get out your notebook and get ready to take notes.

Positive and negative examples:

Student takes out notebook and pen right away.

Student waits 20 seconds and then takes out notebook and pen.

Student takes out notebook but can't find pen.

Student takes out notebook and then talks to friend.

Define • Expectations

reference

See *DSC*, pp. 89–128

TO DO

Use the CHAMPs or ACHIEVE Classroom Activity Worksheets on pp. 8–9 to identify your expectations. Prepare to teach students appropriate behaviors for:

- Major Classroom Activities (e.g., teacher-directed instruction, independent seatwork, class discussions, cooperative group work)
- Transition Times

HOW TO USE THE CHAMPS AND ACHIEVE CLASSROOM ACTIVITY WORKSHEETS

1. Copy the worksheet on p. 8 (CHAMPs) or p. 9 (ACHIEVE) in this planner.
2. Work through the worksheet for each activity. Visualize what you want your classroom activities to look and sound like. Your expectations should describe how students behave during a successful activity.
3. As needed, also define and teach expectations for other activities, such as working in cooperative groups, working in centers, test taking, assemblies, etc.

samples

Exhibit 4.3
**CHAMPs Classroom Activity Worksheet:
Reproducible Template**

Activity: __Independent Seatwork__

CONVERSATION

Can students engage in conversation with each other during this activity? *Yes. Voice Level 1 only.*

If yes, about what? *Questions about work assignments.*

With whom? *Only students they sit next to.*

How many students can be involved in a single conversation? *Only two students.*

How long can the conversation last? *About a minute.*

HELP

How do students get questions answered? How do students get your attention?
Put out Help sign and mark question for when teacher gets to you.

If students have to wait for help, what should they do while they wait?
Students will continue to work on the remainder of the assignment.

ACTIVITY

What is the expected end product of this activity? (This may vary from day to day.)
Completing the assignment.

MOVEMENT

Can students get out of their seats during the activity? *Yes.*

If yes, acceptable reasons include:
Pencil *Yes*   Restroom *Yes, after signing out*
Drink *Yes*   Hand in/pick up materials *Yes*
Other

Do they need permission from you? *Only for the restroom.*

PARTICIPATION

What behaviors show that students are participating fully and responsibly?
Looking at paper. Writing or doing what task requires. Talking only to help or get help.

What behaviors show that a student is not participating?

Talking during movement. Wandering around the room. Looking somewhere other than at work. Not doing task.

Exhibit 4.4
**ACHIEVE Classroom Activity Worksheet:
Reproducible Template**

Achieve—To succeed in something!

Activity (for example, lecture, labs, independent work, tests, cooperative groups)
Independent Seatwork

Conversation

Can students talk to each other? *Yes.*

If so, about what? *Only to get help on the assigned work.*

To whom? *Anyone close. Use a whisper or quiet conversational voice.*

How many can be involved? *No more than three people total.*

How long should conversations last? *No more than a couple of minutes.*

Help

How should students get questions answered during this activity?
Ask another student or ask the teacher.
How should students get your attention?
Place an open book upright on the desk, facing away from you if it's not a book you need.

Integrity   *Keep working.*

What are your expectations for students working together, quoting sources, and so forth? In other words, define what you consider to be, for example, cheating or not cheating, plagiarizing or not plagiarizing.
Do your own work. Help with a few questions is fine. Copying someone else's work is not OK.

Effort

What behaviors would demonstrate active participation? *Reading, writing briefly asking or answering a question about the assigned task.*
What behaviors would demonstrate a lack of participation? *Doing nothing, sleeping, doing work from another class before work on the assigned task is completed.*

Value

How would active participation be of benefit for students? *Doing as much as possible in class will help you identify questions while the teacher is available to help.*

Efficiency

Can you provide tips to increase student productivity?
Avoid becoming distracted. When you complete one task or question, move immediately to the next one. You can connect your mind to the task and get done in a fraction of the time it would require if you let you mind wander to other things.

FIND IT   See pp. 8 and 9 for blank reproducible masters.

Teach • Expectations

TO DO Prepare lessons for teaching your CHAMPs or ACHIEVE expectations.

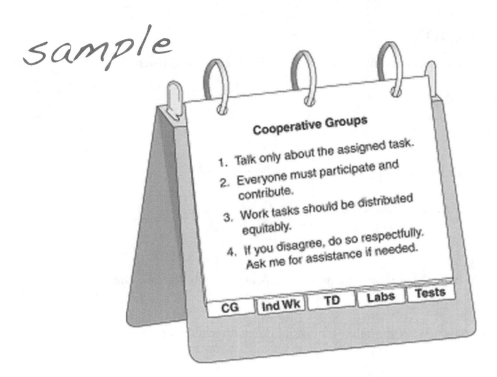

sample

Cooperative Groups

1. Talk only about the assigned task.
2. Everyone must participate and contribute.
3. Work tasks should be distributed equitably.
4. If you disagree, do so respectfully. Ask me for assistance if needed.

CG | Ind Wk | TD | Labs | Tests

Plan to teach by:

1. Telling students what type of activity they will participate in next.
2. Telling students what you expect and showing the CHAMPs or ACHIEVE expectations using a visual display such as the notebook flip chart shown above.
3. Modeling the behaviors you expect to see, with particular emphasis on Participation.
4. Having some students demonstrate the expectations.
5. Modeling some things not to do.
6. Modeling the correct way one more time.
7. Verifying that students understand the expectations. If needed, also plan to clarify expectations by:
   - ✓ Modeling a range of behaviors and having students identify whether you are exhibiting appropriate or inappropriate behavior.
   - ✓ Reviewing all the positive expectations and re-modeling the right way.
8. Having students get started on the activity or transition.

Plan to observe • Have students start on the activity. (Circulate and scan.)

Plan to provide feedback • During and after the activity, provide positive descriptive feedback and corrective feedback.

Exhibit 4.3
CHAMPs Classroom Activity Worksheet: Reproducible Template

Activity: _____

CONVERSATION

Can students engage in conversation with each other during this activity?

If yes, about what?

With whom?

How many students can be involved in a single conversation?

How long can the conversation last?

HELP

How do students get questions answered? How do students get your attention?

If students have to wait for help, what should they do while they wait?

ACTIVITY

What is the expected end product of this activity? (This may vary from day to day.)

MOVEMENT

Can students get out of their seats during the activity?

If yes, acceptable reasons include:
Pencil	Restroom
Drink	Hand in/pick up materials
Other	

Do they need permission from you?

PARTICIPATION

What behaviors show that students are participating fully and responsibly?

What behaviors show that a student is not participating?

≫ *also found on the DSC DVD*

Exhibit 4.4
ACHIEVE Classroom Activity Worksheet: Reproducible Template

Achieve—To succeed in something!

Activity (for example, lecture, labs, independent work, tests, cooperative groups)

Conversation

Can students talk to each other?

If so, about what?

To whom?

How many can be involved?

How long should conversations last?

Help

How should students get questions answered during this activity?

How should students get your attention?

Integrity

What are your expectations for students working together, quoting sources, and so forth? In other words, define what you consider to be, for example, cheating or not cheating, plagiarizing or not plagiarizing.

Effort

What behaviors would demonstrate active participation?

What behaviors would demonstrate a lack of participation?

Value

How would active participation be of benefit for students?

Efficiency

Can you provide tips to increase student productivity?

Define • Grading System

reference

See *DSC*, pp. 27–48

In addition to clearly defined and taught behavioral expectations, the way you organize instructional content and evaluate student mastery of that content can play a major role in whether students have a high or low expectancy of success. A well-designed grading system can also increase students' motivation to engage with course content.

1. *Develop clear long-range goals for each class you teach.*
2. *Design instruction and evaluation procedures that create a clear relationship between student effort and success.*
   - ✓ Clarify the most important objectives of the class and evaluate students only on the basis of those objectives.
   - ✓ Grade students based on their mastery of the objectives, not on a standard curve.
   - ✓ Determine the percentage of mastery that will be used to determine student grades (i.e., 90 percent or better = A; 80–89.9 percent = B, etc.)
3. *Establish a system to provide feedback on behavior and effort.* Incorporate this into your grading system.
   - ✓ Establish a grade percentage for classroom behavior/effort.
   - ✓ Determine the approximate total number of points students may earn during the term.
   - ✓ Determine the approximate total number of points based on behavior and effort.
   - ✓ Design an efficient system for monitoring and recording daily classroom behavior points, such as the Behavior Record Form shown on the next page.
   - ✓ Determine the impact of excused and unexcused absences on your grading of behavior and effort.
   - ✓ Assign weekly performance points and provide feedback to students.
4. *Design procedures for students to receive feedback on each aspect of their behavioral and academic performance and to know their current grades.* Exhibit 2.5 (*DSC*, p. 48) at right is an example of a grading sheet students can use to keep track of their standing in class.

samples

Name	Fri.	Mon.	Tues.	Wed.	Thurs.	Total
						14
Andersen, Gina	dd	EE	dB	d	B	20
Bendix, Frank	E	E	BB	B	R	16
Bigornia, Brad	o					
Collias, Zona	t	B-				

Exhibit 2.5
Student Grading Sheet

CLASS PERIOD _____

STUDENT _____

TESTS:
1 Score _____/100 points
2 Score _____/100 points
3 Score _____/100 points
4 Score _____/100 points
5 Score _____/100 points
Total _____/ 500 points

QUIZZES:
1 Score _____/ 20 points
2 Score _____/ 20 points
3 Score _____/ 20 points
4 Score _____/ 20 points
5 Score _____/ 20 points
Total _____/ 100 points

TERM PAPER:
Score _____/200 points
Total _____/ 200 points

HOMEWORK:
1 Score _____/ 10 points
2 Score _____/ 10 points
3 Score _____/ 10 points
4 Score _____/ 10 points
5 Score _____/ 10 points
6 Score _____/ 10 points
7 Score _____/ 10 points
8 Score _____/ 10 points
9 Score _____/ 10 points
10 Score _____/ 10 points
Total _____/ 100 points

WEEKLY PARTICIPATION:
Week 1 _____/ 20 points
Week 2 _____/ 20 points
Week 3 _____/ 20 points
Week 4 _____/ 20 points
Week 5 _____/ 20 points
Week 6 _____/ 20 points
Week 7 _____/ 20 points
Week 8 _____/ 20 points
Week 9 _____/ 20 points
Total _____/ 180 points

FINAL SCORE _____/1,080 points

Sample of Codes for Behavioral Grading

Misbehavior	Code	Positive Trait	Code
Off task	o	Doing your best (effort)	E
Talking (at the wrong time)	t	Be responsible	B
Disruptive	d	Respect/cooperation	R

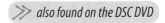 *also found on the DSC DVD*

Exhibit 2.2
Behavior Record Form

Date _____   Reminders _____

Name	Fri.	Mon.	Tues.	Wed.	Thurs.	Total

Codes:

Set Up • The Classroom Management Plan and Syllabus

reference

See *DSC*, pp. 165–168

TO DO Read the information below and/or on pp. 165–168 in *Discipline in the Secondary Classroom*. Then complete the Syllabus Template on pp. 11–13 of this planner.

Once you've clarified behavioral expectations and designed your grading system, you can complete your Classroom Management Plan and course syllabus.

1. ***Make a copy of the Syllabus Template on pp. 11–13 of this planner.*** (*DSC* Exhibit 7.1 has been modified to provide more room for notes.)

2. ***Plan an attention signal.***
   Determine how you will get students' attention with an auditory and visual signal.

3. ***Plan to encourage students.***
   Teach with enthusiasm and effective practices.
   Provide noncontingent attention to each student throughout the day.
   Provide positive contingent feedback to the student and class when appropriate academic and/or behavioral performance is demonstrated.
   Be aware of your ratios of interactions. With each student, you should have at least three positive interactions to every corrective interaction.

4. ***Plan to correct misbehavior.***
   When a rule is broken, deliver *mild* consequences consistently, appropriately, and unemotionally. Interact with the student immediately, briefly, and without arguing.
   Respond to early-stage misbehavior by using proximity management, gentle verbal reprimands, discussion, family contact, humor, or restitution.
   Respond to later-stage misbehavior with mild consequences such as loss of points, time owed, timeout (in the classroom, in another class), restitution, detention, or demerits.
   For severe misbehavior, refer the student to the office.

5. ***Finalize your classroom management plan and prepare to communicate it to your students.***
   Work through the Syllabus Template on the next three pages. Then compare your plan to the sample syllabus in *DSC*, pp. 168–171. Do you have policies and procedures clearly articulated in each section of the template? Use the template references to *DSC* for additional information and revise as needed. Once you've completed the template, prepare a student syllabus for each course you teach. The student syllabus may not be as detailed as the completed template, but your advance thinking on all variables will help you define your policies and procedures.

NONCONTINGENT ATTENTION

Noncontingent attention is a fancy way of saying that you will give attention to every student regardless of his or her academic or behavioral success. These friendly interactions help every student feel valued.

TIMEOUT

Timeout can be an effective later-stage consequence if it is dull and uninteresting. Rather than being aversive, an effective timeout removes the student from an opportunity to participate in more interesting activities.

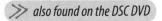

also found on the DSC DVD

DSC Exhibit 7.1
Syllabus Template

Classroom Goals
Write your classroom goals in the form of what students will be able to successfully do at the end of the year or semester. See *DSC*, Chapter Two, Task 1.

Guidelines for Success
Write your list of attitudes and traits that you feel will ensure your students' success. See *DSC*, Chapter One, Task 5.

Classroom Rules
Outline the important student behaviors that will ensure your class runs efficiently. See *DSC*, Chapter Five, Task 1.

Activities
Outline the activities that students will be engaging in during a typical week. See *DSC*, Chapter Four, Task 1.

Grades
Grading scale: Outline the percentage cutoffs for A's, B's, and so on.
Relative value: Outline the relative weight of homework, quizzes, tests, papers, and behavior and effort on the final grade.
See *DSC*, Chapter Two, Tasks 2 to 4.

Classroom Procedures
Entering the classroom
Outline exactly what students should do from the time they enter the room until the bell rings for class to begin.
See *DSC*, Chapter Three, Task 4.

Continued

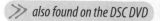

Syllabus Template (continued)

Tardy to class
Provide your definition of on time and tardy, and identify the consequences for being tardy.
See *DSC*, Chapter Three, Task 4.

Paper or pencil
Identify what students should have to write with. In addition, specify what a student should do if he or she does not have this and what, if anything, you implement as a consequence. See *DSC*, Chapter Three, Task 4.

How to find out what the daily assignments are
Identify how you will assign work and how students will know what they are to do each day. Also define how they should keep track of what they need to do for homework and long-range assignments. See *DSC*, Chapter Three, Task 5.

Turning in assignments
Identify where and how students turn in class work and homework. Specify if students are to check off completed work they have turned in. See *DSC*, Chapter Three, Task 5.

Returning assignments to students
Detail your policies on how you will return completed work to your students. See *DSC*, Chapter Three, Task 5.

Finding out grade status
Review your grading system, and explain whether you will give students a weekly grade report or if you expect them to track their grades themselves. Also identify when and how a student can approach you to discuss his or her current status in the class. See *DSC*, Chapter Two, Task 4.

Continued

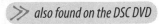

Syllabus Template (continued)

Student responsibilities after an absence

Outline what students will need to do when returning after an absence.

- How to find out what they missed
- How long they have to make up assignments
- What to do if they miss a test

See *DSC*, Chapter Three, Task 5.

Late, missing, or incomplete assignments

Outline the maximum number of late assignments you will accept, along with penalties and time limits for late work. See *DSC*, Chapter Three, Task 5.

Communication procedures with parents and families

Identify if you will have any regular communication with families that you initiate. Provide information on when, where, and how family members can get in touch with you.

Ending class

Specify how you will end class, any responsibilities your students may have, and how you will dismiss the students. See *DSC*, Chapter Three, Task 4.

Consequences for Classroom Rule Violations

List the range of corrective consequences that you may assign if rules are violated. See *DSC*, Chapter Five, Task 3.

Consequences for Code of Conduct Violations

Inform students that you must follow through with disciplinary referrals for violations of schoolwide rules, including dress code, unexcused absences, threats, and so forth. Make sure to get this information from your principal or assistant principal.

Reflect • Grade Book Analysis

reference

See *DSC*, pp. 257–259

Before the end of each grading period, review data on absenteeism, tardiness, work completion, and assignment failure. This information will help you determine whether an individual student or class would benefit from a behavior management plan. Analysis of these variables will also help you share information with parents and staff who have a role in developing and implementing student support plans.

Note: If you use a computerized grade book, this information may already be summarized for you.

TO DO

Review the Grade Book Analysis Worksheet on the next page.

WHEN: Write reminders in your lesson planner to complete this worksheet before the end of each grading period.

HOW TO USE THE GRADE BOOK ANALYSIS WORKSHEET

sample

1. Gather data on:
   - ✓ Percentage of attendance
   - ✓ Percentage of days on time
   - ✓ Percentage of in-class work completion
   - ✓ Percentage of quality work
   - ✓ Current grade status (to identify students who may need targeted academic assistance)

2. Copy the Grade Book Analysis Worksheet on the next page and enter data for each student. (See *DSC*, pp. 257–259, for instructions.)

3. Analyze your results by looking for patterns of behavior. Students should be at or above 95 percent in attendance, punctuality, work completion, and homework completion. They should be passing all subjects.

Does your data indicate a problem with your class or with individuals?

   - ✓ If one or two students fail to meet one of these goals, look at the interrelationships between factors. Then design individual action plans to change the behavior. You may wish to consult with parents, school administrators, nurses, counselors, or the school psychologist.
   - ✓ If three or more students fail to meet a goal, consider a whole-class intervention.

Exhibit D.1
Grade Book Analysis Worksheet

Teacher __Ms. Lloyd__   Date ___11/4___

Student Name or Number	% Attendance	% Punctuality	% Work Completion	% Quality Work	Overall Grade Status
Alexander, R.	90	98	100	95	89
Bailey, S.	65	90	55	50	59
Coleman, E.	90	100	90	95	87
Diaz, A.	100	75	100	98	96
Jackson, L.	95	100	95	90	85
Lewis, M.	95	100	100	100	93
Miller, T.	100	100	98	100	95
Murphy, C.	100	95	90	95	80
Parker, A.	100	80	100	100	95
Perez, D.	90	95	100	98	78
Price, H.	95	95	100	98	79
Robinson, I.	100	100	95	100	92
Ross, O.	60	80	85	88	79
Simmons, P.	100	95	98	95	87
Thomas, L.	95	95	96	98	86
Torres, U.	90	95	95	90	87
Washington, K.	100	95	100	90	98
White, S.	100	70	100	100	97
Wilson, D.	100	98	100	90	96

Analysis and Plan of Action

1st Period—Introductory Calculus

S. Bailey and O. Ross fall below expectations on all variables. S. Bailey is a recent transfer student. Ms. Lloyd will assess skills and explore options for tutoring to catch up. A. Diaz, A. Parker, O. Ross, and S. White are often tardy because of a late-arriving bus. Ms. Lloyd decides to discuss the problem with the administration. In the meantime, she will begin the class with a short independent work period and then move to instruction. Ms. Lloyd will also work with O. Ross on attendance issues with problem-solving and goal setting.

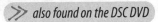

Exhibit D.1
Grade Book Analysis Worksheet

Teacher _____ Date _____

Student Name or Number	% Attendance	% Punctuality	% Work Completion	% Quality Work	Overall Grade Status

Week of

NOTES

TIME	**MONDAY**	**TUESDAY**

Interact positively.

Noncontingent [positive] attention involves interacting with students not because of anything they've done but just because you notice and value them as people.

Week of

NOTES

TIME

Correct minor misbehavior calmly and consistently.

WEDNESDAY	THURSDAY	FRIDAY

Student misbehavior is an instructional opportunity.

NOTES

MONDAY

TUESDAY

TIME

Observe!

WEDNESDAY	THURSDAY	FRIDAY

Circulate through your classroom whenever possible • Scan frequently • By monitoring student behavior, you will have many opportunities to provide positive and corrective feedback. This will teach students responsible and productive work habits.

Verify • Student Understanding

reference

See *DSC*, pp. 189–195

During the second or third week of school, make sure your students understand your behavioral expectations. Student quizzes can help you decide whether to continue teaching expectations. This process also communicates to students how important it is to know and understand your expectations for classroom behavior and safety.

TO DO

Design an age-appropriate quiz on your behavioral expectations. Analyze the results and re-teach as needed.

WHEN: Week 3

TIPS FOR DESIGNING A QUIZ

1. Design a short quiz (see the example on the next page). Use a familiar format—true/false, multiple choice, fill in the blank, short essay, or a mix of formats.
2. Determine the content of the quiz by examining your ACHIEVE or CHAMPs expectations. Target complex activities and transitions that give students the most difficulty.
3. Prepare your students to take the quiz. Tell students that the quiz will not be graded. Explain the purpose—to help you determine whether you should re-teach your expectations and provide additional practice.
4. Re-teach expectations as needed.

STUDENT QUIZZES

A written quiz is a quick, simple way to determine if all your students know your expectations and rules.

Don't assume that students are willful when they don't follow the rules. Make sure your students fully understand your expectations and rules.
Teach and re-teach!

Exhibit 8.1

Sample Quiz on Expectations

Name _Brandi Carson_   Date _10/2_

Circle the letter for the best answer to each question.

1. When you enter the classroom and begin working on the challenge problem . . .
   a. you should be completely silent from the moment you enter the room.
   (b.) you can talk quietly as you enter, but must be silent when you take your seat.
   c. you can talk quietly about anything, but when the bell rings, you should be in your seat and then you can talk only about the challenge problem on the overhead projector.
   d. you can talk loudly about anything, but when the bell rings, you should get to your seat within two minutes and then get quiet.

2. During class, you can use the pencil sharpener . . .
   a. only before and after class.
   (b.) before and after class and during independent work periods.
   c. any time you need to.
   d. at no time without teacher permission.

3. When the teacher gives the attention signal and you should . . .
   (a.) be silent and have your eyes on the teacher
   b. be silent and have your eyes on the teacher
   c. be silent and have your eyes on the teacher
   d. loudly tell other students to be quiet and pa

4. During the time the teacher is speaking to the c
   a. talk quietly to someone near you and get ou pencil.
   b. talk quietly to someone near you and not g
   c. talk only if you have been called on by the you need a drink of water or supplies.
   (d.) talk only if you have been called on by the seat without permission.

5. Active participation while the teacher is prese certain way. Circle any of the items that descr correct answers.
   (a.) Sit up straight or lean forward.
   (b.) Raise your hand if you have something to

   (c.) Answer questions when called on.
   d. Write notes to your friends.
   (e.) Write notes to keep in your binder that will help you study for tests.
   f. Tell people who are talking that they need to shut up and listen.
   g. Have toys and things on your desk that will help entertain you during the lesson.
   (h.) Keep your eyes on the person speaking or on the class notes you are writing.
   i. Let your mind wander.
   j. Talk while the teacher is talking.
   (k.) Be respectful toward the teacher and other students in what you say and how you act.
   l. Call out answers to questions.
   m. Be vocal with your opinion.
   n. Actively discuss the lesson.

6. When you return after an absence, you should . . .
   a. ask the teacher, "Did I miss anything while I was gone?"
   b. ask another student for his or her notes.
   (c.) go to the file by the drinking fountain and find the folder for this class period and take the copied pages for the days you were absent.
   d. go to the teacher's desk and open her plan book to the dates you missed and copy all the important information.

7. In the parentheses after each of the following statements, put a **T** if the concept is true and an **F** if the concept is false about the weekly points you earn for behavior and effort.
   a. Every student starts the week with 10 out of 20 possible points. (T)
   b. Every reminder the teacher gives you about your behavior or effort in class costs 1 point. (T)
   c. Every compliment the teacher gives you about your behavior or effort in class adds 1 point. (T)
   d. These points are added into the grade book and are part of your academic grade. (F)
   e. The teacher will take points away, without informing you about each incident. (F)
   f. For severe misbehavior, you can have a choice between an office referral or a loss of points. (F)
   g. You can make an appointment to discuss anything you do not understand or think is unfair about this system. (T)

sample

> Good classroom management is about teaching and re-teaching your expectations.

NOTES

TIME

MONDAY

TUESDAY

Know your academic objectives.

WEDNESDAY	THURSDAY	FRIDAY

Determine the criteria by which you will evaluate the end product. By settling on your final evaluation tool first, you can then identify exactly what you want students to know or be able to do and then determine the essential content you will teach them.

NOTES

TIME	**MONDAY**	**TUESDAY**

Teach and re-teach your expectations.

WEDNESDAY	THURSDAY	FRIDAY

When you teach students how to behave responsibly, you dramatically increase their productivity • Demonstrate and discuss your expectations and provide positive practice.

Double-Check • Expectations and Behavior

reference

See *DSC*, pp. 233–241

During the second or third week of school, you gave your students quizzes to determine how well they *understood* your expectations. With the CHAMPs or ACHIEVE versus Daily Reality Rating Scale, you can now determine the degree to which student behavior *matches* your expectations. This information will help you pinpoint specific activities, transitions, and times when expectations need to be re-taught. This process will also help you determine whether to implement a classwide or individual interventions to encourage more appropriate student behavior.

TO DO

Complete a Daily Reality Rating Scale and analyze the data. Re-teach as needed.

WHEN: Week 4 or 5, and shortly after winter break

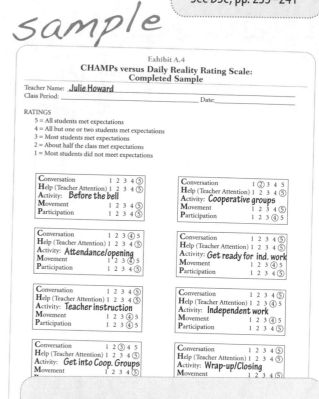

sample

Exhibit A.4
CHAMPs versus Daily Reality Rating Scale: Completed Sample

Teacher Name: Julie Howard
Class Period: _____ Date: _____

RATINGS
5 = All students met expectations
4 = All but one or two students met expectations
3 = Most students met expectations
2 = About half the class met expectations
1 = Most students did not meet expectations

Analysis and Plan of Action

4th Period—History

Only one activity (Cooperative Groups) and one transition (Getting into Cooperative Groups) have ratings lower than 4 and 5. These ratings indicate that students are talking too loudly, making the noise level in the room excessive. Mrs. Howard decides to keep the class at a low level of structure, but she plans to re-teach her expectations with particular emphasis on how students can monitor and manage voice levels within their cooperative groups.

HOW TO USE THE DAILY REALITY RATING SCALE

1. Make a copy of ACHIEVE versus Daily Reality Rating Scale on the next page. See *DSC*, Appendix A, for the CHAMPs rating scale shown at right.

2. Choose one or more class periods in which student behavior tends to be most problematic.

3. Identify major activities and transitions that occur during the class period. Write each one on an Activity line in one of the form's rating boxes.

4. Before each activity or transition, briefly review your expectations with students. Immediately after completing the activity or transition, rate the degree to which students met your expectations.

5. Review the data to determine which expectations may require re-teaching. If the behavior of one or two specific students concerns you, consider an individual behavior management plan (*DSC*, Chapter 9).

If students score ratings of 4 or 5 in . . .	Then . . .
All activities and transitions	Keep doing what you are doing.
60–70 percent of all activities and transitions	Re-teach expectations and procedures outlined in your syllabus, as needed. Consider increasing the level of class structure. See *DSC*, p. 18.
59 percent or fewer of all activities and transitions	Implement a classwide system. See *DSC*, pp. 203–228. Re-teach expectations and procedures outlined in your syllabus, as needed. Consider increasing the level of class structure. See *DSC*, p. 18.

Exhibit A.5
ACHIEVE versus Daily Reality Rating Scale: Reproducible Form

Teacher Name: _____

Class Period: _____ Date: _____

RATINGS

    5 = All students met expectations
    4 = All but one or two students met expectations
    3 = Most students met expectations
    2 = About half the class met expectations
    1 = Most students did not meet expectations

Activity:	
Conversation	1 2 3 4 5
Help	1 2 3 4 5
Integrity	1 2 3 4 5
Effort	1 2 3 4 5
Value	1 2 3 4 5
Efficiency	1 2 3 4 5

Activity:	
Conversation	1 2 3 4 5
Help	1 2 3 4 5
Integrity	1 2 3 4 5
Effort	1 2 3 4 5
Value	1 2 3 4 5
Efficiency	1 2 3 4 5

Activity:	
Conversation	1 2 3 4 5
Help	1 2 3 4 5
Integrity	1 2 3 4 5
Effort	1 2 3 4 5
Value	1 2 3 4 5
Efficiency	1 2 3 4 5

Activity:	
Conversation	1 2 3 4 5
Help	1 2 3 4 5
Integrity	1 2 3 4 5
Effort	1 2 3 4 5
Value	1 2 3 4 5
Efficiency	1 2 3 4 5

Activity:	
Conversation	1 2 3 4 5
Help	1 2 3 4 5
Integrity	1 2 3 4 5
Effort	1 2 3 4 5
Value	1 2 3 4 5
Efficiency	1 2 3 4 5

Activity:	
Conversation	1 2 3 4 5
Help	1 2 3 4 5
Integrity	1 2 3 4 5
Effort	1 2 3 4 5
Value	1 2 3 4 5
Efficiency	1 2 3 4 5

Transition 1:

Transition 2:

Transition 3:

Week of

NOTES

TIME	MONDAY	TUESDAY

Structure your classroom for success.

WEDNESDAY	THURSDAY	FRIDAY

Review your routines: Are they well organized and efficient? • When you have well-organized routines and procedures for your classroom, you model and prompt organized behavior from your students.

Week of

TIME	MONDAY	TUESDAY

Observe activities and transitions.

WEDNESDAY	THURSDAY	FRIDAY

Are there activities that don't run as smoothly as you would like? • Are there activities you haven't defined and taught expectations for (e.g., partner work, assemblies, entering the classroom . . .)? • If yes, define your expectations and then teach and re-teach them.

Evaluate • Ratio of Interactions

reference

See *DSC*, pp. 243–250

A high ratio of positive to negative interactions with students has been shown to improve student motivation and academic performance while reducing disrespect, disruptions, and other misbehaviors. The Ratio of Interactions Monitoring Form will help you determine whether your interactions with students are primarily positive or whether you have fallen into the Criticism Trap. The Criticism Trap occurs when a teacher pays more attention to student misbehavior than to responsible behavior. Some students will misbehave to get the teacher's attention. Though misbehavior stops for the moment, over time the misbehavior occurs more and more frequently. The Ratio of Interactions Monitoring Form gives a snapshot of what is happening in your classes.

TO DO

Monitor your interactions using the Ratio of Interactions Monitoring Form. Your goal is to have a ratio of at least three positive interactions to every negative interaction.

WHEN: During the second month of school and again in early to mid-February

HOW TO USE THE RATIO OF INTERACTIONS MONITORING FORM

1. Copy the Ratio of Interactions Monitoring Form on the next page. See *DSC*, Appendix B, for other versions.

2. Make sure you understand the following:
   - ✓ If student behavior is appropriate at the time of the interaction, the interaction is positive.
   - ✓ If the behavior is inappropriate at the time of the interaction, it is negative. That is, if misbehavior prompts the interaction—regardless of your tone or what you say—the interaction is negative.

3. Determine the class periods during which you have the most trouble being positive with students. Arrange to audio or video record those periods.

4. Listen to or watch the recording and mark your interactions on the form. Tally each positive and negative interaction with a student or the class. You can also assign codes to track interactions with a particular student or in regard to a particular behavior.

5. Calculate and analyze your ratio of positive to negative interactions. Did you achieve at least a 3:1 ratio?

6. If needed, work on increasing positive interactions and decreasing negative interactions. Read *DSC*, pp. 156–158, and review the Planner Tips for ways to increase positive interactions. Repeat this activity in a few weeks.

sample

Exhibit B.1
Ratio of Interactions Monitoring Form During a Particular Time of Day: Reproducible Form

Teacher: **Mrs. Hammond**   Date: **10/12**

Student's Name: _____

Coding System:

M = Male
F = Female
N = Nick
C = Class

Attention to Positive	Attention to Negative
M, M, M, F, M, F	N, N, M, N, F, F, N
F, C, F, N, F, M	N, C, M, M, N
C. M. M. N, F. M	

Analysis and Plan of Action

3rd Period—Language Arts

The overall ratio of interactions is 1.5:1 (18:12). However, when the interactions with one student (Nick) are removed, the ratio is close to 3:1. Interactions with Nick are primarily negative (1:3 ratio). The teacher will work on minimizing the attention paid to Nick's problem behavior (talking during class) and increasing positive interactions with him. She will also make a note to provide the entire class with positive feedback after every activity.

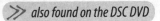

Exhibit B.1

Ratio of Interactions Monitoring Form During a
Particular Time of Day: Reproducible Form

Teacher: _____   Date: _____

Student's Name: _____

Coding System:

Attention to Positive	Attention to Negative

Analysis and Plan of Action:

NOTES

TIME	**MONDAY**	**TUESDAY**

Interact positively. Catch students being successful.

WEDNESDAY	THURSDAY	FRIDAY

Maintain a focus on responsible behavior • Tell students what they are doing right and how these behaviors will help them meet your school's Guidelines for Success and be successful in the future—at work, in college, and in achieving long-range goals.

NOTES

MONDAY

TUESDAY

TIME

Teach with highly interactive lessons.

WEDNESDAY	THURSDAY	FRIDAY

The more students do something that engages them with the lesson content, the greater their chance to learn the essential content.

Analyze • Patterns of Misbehavior

reference

See *DSC*, pp. 251–256

Is misbehavior causing disruptions in your classroom? If the answer is yes, use the Misbehavior Recording Sheet to help analyze patterns of misbehavior. You will identify:

✓ What misbehaviors are occurring

✓ How often misbehavior is occurring

✓ Who is misbehaving

Data will help you determine whether you need to implement an intervention plan or targeted plans to improve specific types of student behavior.

TO DO

Collect and record data on student misbehavior using a Misbehavior Recording Sheet.

WHEN: Early part of third month of school and in mid- to late January, or as needed

sample

Exhibit C.1
Misbehavior Recording Sheet: Student Name

Date 11/4 Reminders _on Wed., remind about Friday test_
Class Period 2

Name	Mon.	Tues.	Wed.	Thurs.	Fri.	Total
Anderson, Chantel				T		1
Bahena, Ruben						0
Bell, Justin						0
Carrouza, Melinda		T		T	T	3
Cummings, Teresa						0
Demalski, Lee			T			1
Diaz, Margo						0
Etienne, Jerry						0
Fujiyama, Kim						0
Grover, Matthew	DDT	DO		DT	T	8
Henry, Scott						0
Isaacson, Chris				D		1
Kaufman, Jamie						0
King, Mark				T		1
LaRouche, Janel				T		1
Morales, Maria Louisa						0
Narlin, Jenny			O	O		2
Neely, Jakob						0
Nguyen, Trang						9
Ogden, Todd	TTD	D	OO	T	TT	0
Pallant, Jared						0
Piercey, Dawn			T	O	T	3
Reaves, Myra						0
Thomason, Rahsaan	TT		T	T	TT	6
Vandever, Aaron						0
Wong, Charlene						0
Yamamota, James		T		OT		3

HOW TO USE THE MISBEHAVIOR RECORDING SHEET

1. Copy the Misbehavior Recording Sheet on the next page. Add student names. See *DSC*, Appendix C, for a seating-chart version of this form.

2. Put the Misbehavior Recording Sheet on a clipboard so you can keep it with you and record data.

3. Tell students that you will record incidents of misbehavior during the week.

4. Use a coding system to record misbehavior whenever you have to correct a student or the group.

5. Analyze the data and determine a plan of action. If misbehavior is infrequent, no action may be required. If you are concerned about the amount of misbehavior, identify the two or three students who misbehaved most frequently. Determine the percentage of total class misbehavior attributable to them. If that percentage is:

✓ More than 90 percent, keep your class structure as is and consider implementing individual behavior management plans.

✓ 60 to 89 percent, re-teach your expectations for a few days, then once a week for another months. Also consider implementing individual behavior management plans for the students who misbehave the most.

✓ Less than 60 percent, consider implementing high structure for this class. Re-teach your expectations for a few days, then once a week for another months. Also consider adding a classwide system (*DSC*, Chapter 9).

Analysis and Plan of Action

6th Period—Physical Science

Scott Henry, Todd Ogden, and Rahsaan Thomason are the students who misbehave the most—the three totaled 23 misbehaviors during this week, or 64% of the total class misbehavior. The teacher will develop individual behavior management plans for these three students and re-teach expectations, with a particular focus on Conversation and Participation.

CODE FOR MISBEHAVIOR

O = Off task

B = Bothering others

T = Talking

D = Disrupting

S = Out of seat

A = Arguing

Code any other common misbehaviors you wish to monitor.

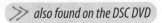

Exhibit C.1
Misbehavior Recording Sheet: Student Name

Date _____   Reminders _____

Class Period _____

Name	Mon.	Tues.	Wed.	Thurs.	Fri.	Total

Codes:

NOTES

TIME	MONDAY	TUESDAY

Correct and teach.

WEDNESDAY	THURSDAY	FRIDAY

When you treat student misbehavior as an instructional opportunity, you give students the chance to learn from their mistakes • For every correction, make sure you interact with the student at least three times while the student is behaving responsibly.

Week of

MONDAY

TUESDAY

TIME

Implement consequences consistently.

WEDNESDAY	THURSDAY	FRIDAY

You must strive to implement corrective consequences unemotionally so your reactions do not give any students the idea that they can have power over you by misbehaving. Clear rules and consistent corrective consequences will reduce, and eventually eliminate, the majority of classroom misbehavior.

Week of

NOTES

TIME

Teach with well-paced lessons.

WEDNESDAY	THURSDAY	FRIDAY

Give students many opportunities to respond • Active response methods include choral responses, taking notes, using framed outlines, filling in graphic organizers, and quick, ungraded quizzes.

NOTES

TIME	MONDAY	TUESDAY

Consult with colleagues.

WEDNESDAY	THURSDAY	FRIDAY

Collegial problem-solving is a powerful mechanism for getting ideas about ways to help students • If you have a student with significant behavioral challenges, it is especially important to consult with colleagues.

Week of

NOTES

_____
_____
_____
_____
_____
_____
_____
_____
_____
_____
_____
_____
_____
_____
_____
_____
_____
_____
_____
_____
_____
_____
_____
_____
_____
_____
_____
_____

TIME

MONDAY

TUESDAY

Structure for success.

WEDNESDAY	THURSDAY	FRIDAY

Make sure your room layout allows you to circulate so you can provide corrective feedback to students who are off task, give positive feedback to students who are using their work time well, and answer the questions of students who need assistance.

NOTES

TIME

MONDAY	TUESDAY

Build relationships with positive interactions.

Provide noncontingent interactions • Demonstrate an interest in every student • Greet students • Demonstrate an interest in each student's work • Have conversations.

Monitor • On-Task Behavior

reference

See *DSC*, pp. 261–264

The ability to work independently is an important life skill.

Throughout schooling, independent work periods occur frequently and are critical to learning.

Use the On-Task Behavior Observation Sheet to help you:

✓ Determine whether you need to adjust and clarify expectations for independent work.

✓ Determine whether you need to re-teach your expectations for independent work.

✓ Identify possible causes of poor work completion rates.

TO DO

Take data using the On-Task Behavior Observation Sheet. Determine the class average for on-task behavior. Your goal is 90 percent on task.

WHEN: During the fourth month of school and in mid- to late February.

HOW TO USE THE ON-TASK BEHAVIOR OBSERVATION SHEET

1. Copy the On-Task Behavior Observation Sheet (next page).

2. Identify the independent work period that you wish to monitor.

3. Decide whether to observe and collect your own data or have a colleague observe.

4. An observer should:

   ✓ Position herself where it is easy to observe students working at their seats.

   ✓ Choose an observation pattern. (For example, start in the front row and scan from left to right.)

   ✓ Look at the first student for an instant, then record + (plus) for on task or − (minus) for off task.

   ✓ Repeat this pattern for each student.

   ✓ Work through the pattern at least three times so that every student is observed three times.

5. Determine percentage of on-task behavior (divide total number of on-task marks by total number of marks).

6. Analyze the data and determine a plan of action. Share the results with students. If the class average is:

   ✓ More than 90 percent on task, congratulate students. If necessary, set goals for specific students.

   ✓ Between 80 and 89 percent on task, tell the students they did well but there is room for improvement. Work with students on strategies to improve independent work skills. If necessary, set goals and plans for specific students.

   ✓ Below 80 percent, review and revise your expectations for independent work. Tell students that they will be working on improving independent work skills. Re-teach and consider adding a classwide motivation system.

> If students are off task, valuable learning time is lost.

sample

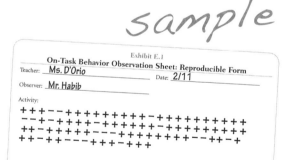

Exhibit E.1
On-Task Behavior Observation Sheet: Reproducible Form
Teacher: Ms. D'Orio   Date: 2/11
Observer: Mr. Habib

Activity:

```
+ + + − − + + + + + + + + − + + + + + + + + +
− − + − + + + − + + + + + − + + + + + + + + +
+ + − + + + + + − − + + + + + − + + + + + + +
+ + − + + − − + + + − + + + + +
```

Analysis and Plan of Action

5th Period—Spanish

This class was on task about 78 percent of the time observed (70/90). Ms. D'Orio will re-teach her expectations for Independent Work and appropriate participation. The class is averaging an 85 percent work completion rate, which indicates that the time devoted to independent work is not excessive. She will also implement goal setting with the two students who displayed the most off-task behavior.

Exhibit E.1

On-Task Behavior Observation Sheet: Reproducible Form

Teacher: _____   Date: _____

Observer: _____

Activity:

Analysis and Plan of Action

NOTES

TIME

MONDAY

TUESDAY

Observe objectively with data.

WEDNESDAY	THURSDAY	FRIDAY

Objective data can help you determine which aspects of your management plan should be maintained, which may need to be altered, and whether your level of structure is adequate • For example, monitor your ratios of interactions • See Planner, pp. 34–35 and 80–81.

Week of

NOTES

TIME	MONDAY	TUESDAY

Take care of yourself.

WEDNESDAY	THURSDAY	FRIDAY

Maintain a positive mindset • Get adequate rest and exercise, and remember to take the time to engage in interests and activities outside of school.

Week of

TIME	MONDAY	TUESDAY

Provide positive descriptive feedback.

WEDNESDAY	THURSDAY	FRIDAY

Use the student's name • Then give a quick description of what the student did—
not just "good job" • Use a quiet voice • Be somewhat businesslike • "Allison, you applied
the formula, performed a series of computations, and came up with the correct answer."

Reflect and Revise •
The Classroom Management Plan

Continuous improvement is an important element of classroom management. Midyear is the perfect time to reflect, review, and modify your classroom management plan. This process will help you determine how to help your students through the rest of the year.

TO DO

Review your classroom management plan and syllabus (see pp. 10–13 in this Planner) and revise accordingly. Circle "Yes" or "No" in response to the questions below.

1. Do any students demonstrate behaviors that keep them from developing positive relationships with peers and adults? **Yes   No**

2. Do any students have academic difficulties due to behavioral issues (e.g., off-task behavior, failure to turn in work, failure to complete homework)? **Yes   No**

3. Are there students who create behavior problems in your classroom? **Yes   No**

4. Are you feeling sick, tired, and frustrated at the end of the day? **Yes   No**

If you answered "Yes" to any of the questions above, this is an especially important process.

HOW TO REVIEW YOUR CLASSROOM MANAGEMENT PLAN AND SYLLABUS

1. ***Classroom Goals:*** Are students on track to achieve their semester and year-end goals?

If no …	• Identify the goals that are proving to be a challenge. Why are they a challenge? • Think about what you are doing that is helping students meet the goals. What is hindering them?	See *DSC,* pp. 28–30

2. ***Guidelines for Success:*** Does behavior reflect your school's Guidelines for Success?

If no …	• Ask whether you need to emphasize specific guidelines. For example, if some students have behaviors that prevent them from working cooperatively with others, you might plan a class discussion. ***This semester, I'd like us to work on our guideline "Be respectful of yourself and others." Let's brainstorm ways we show our respect for others. What are some behaviors that do not show respect?*** • Consider whether you need to overtly teach students how their behavior exemplifies the guidelines. If yes, mentally practice age-appropriate feedback. ***That was good information to share with the group.***	See *DSC,* pp. 16–18

3. ***Classroom Rules:*** Are students following rules with few exceptions?

If yes …	Ask yourself whether to revise a rule or two. For example, if students are arriving on time with all their materials, congratulate them on their maturity and change to a more sophisticated rule such as "Encourage others."	
If no …	• Whether your enforcement of rules is consistent and fair. • Re-teach your rules with visuals, role-plays, and positive practice. • Acknowledge appropriate student behavior more frequently.	See *DSC,* pp. 130–132

4. ***Attention Signal:*** Does your signal result in immediate attention from your students?

If yes …	Continue with your current signal.	
If no …	Change your signal. Teach students the new signal, use it consistently, and acknowledge students who quickly follow your signal.	See *DSC,* pp. 63–64

5. **CHAMPS Expectations for Activities and Transitions:** Are students meeting your expectations?

If yes . . .	Continue to reinforce students with positive descriptive feedback.
If no . . .	• Ask whether your expectations clearly define what activities and transitions should look and sound like. • Revise and then re-teach expectations with visuals, discussions, role-plays, and/or positive practice. Provide frequent positive feedback. • Consider implementing or modifying a classwide system, as discussed in *DSC*, Chapter 9.

See *DSC*, pp. 92–117

6. **Grades:** Do students understand the grading system? Are they always aware of their current grade?

If yes . . .	Continue with existing system.
If no . . .	• Re-teach your grading system and grade monitoring expectations. • If students seem to be having difficulty with one or two aspects of your system, consider modifying or simplifying those areas.

See *DSC*, pp. 31–47

7. **Classroom Procedures:** Do students follow your procedures for entering class, bringing materials, turning in assignments, etc?

If yes . . .	Continue to reinforce students with positive descriptive feedback.
If no . . .	• Ask whether your procedures clearly define what activities and transitions should look and sound like. • Revise and then re-teach procedures with visuals, discussions, role-plays, and/or positive practice. • Provide frequent positive feedback. • Consider implementing or modifying a classwide system, as discussed in *DSC*, Chapter 9.

See *DSC*, pp. 54–63; 69–82

8. **Beginning and Ending Routines:** Are beginning and ending routines efficient and productive?

If yes . . .	Continue to monitor and re-teach as needed.
If no . . .	Revise and re-teach.

See *DSC*, pp. 64–69

9. **Managing Work:** Do your students regularly complete independent work and homework?

If yes . . .	Continue to monitor and re-teach procedures as needed.
If no . . .	• Before assigning independent work, provide explicit instruction—model, guide, and then monitor and assist individuals. • Determine whether students can read work fluently, accurately, and with understanding. Modify assignments. Set up academic intervention plans.

See *DSC*, pp. 72–82

10. **Consequences for Classroom Rule Violations and Code of Conduct Violations:** Do students rarely break rules or engage in misbehavior?

If yes . . .	Continue to enforce rules with mild, calm, and consistent corrections.
If no . . .	• If only one or two students engage in frequent misbehavior, consider modifying your correction procedures for those individuals. For example, you may ignore students disruptions if they are attention-seeking. • If several students are engaging in frequent misbehavior, review and modify your corrective consequences so they are: a) consistent, b) implemented without bias, c) calm, and d) respectful.

See *DSC*, pp. 135–140

Excellence in classroom management is a process of continuous improvement.

NOTES

MONDAY

TUESDAY

TIME

Your grade book is a wealth of data.

WEDNESDAY	THURSDAY	FRIDAY

Look for patterns—by subject, by assignment type (e.g., homework, in-class), and by student •
As you spot trends, adjust the structure of instruction. For example, if students have difficulty completing independent work, provide more teacher-directed instruction before assigning independent work.

NOTES

MONDAY	TUESDAY

TIME

Present tasks to students in a manner that generates enthusiasm.

WEDNESDAY	THURSDAY	FRIDAY

Explain how an activity will be useful to students now and in the future • Provide a vision of what students will eventually be able to accomplish • Relate new tasks to previously learned skills • Don't be afraid to give students a pep talk, especially for challenging tasks.

NOTES

MONDAY

TUESDAY

TIME

Teach with precorrections.

A strategy for preventing misbehavior is to anticipate the problem and then prompt the appropriate behavior before the misbehavior occurs. For example, if you anticipate that students will run out the door when the bell rings, before the bell rings remind students to wait and walk.

Motivate • Enhance Students' Desire to Succeed

reference
See *DSC*, pp. 145–164

Motivating your students can be challenging, but the rewards are worthwhile. When your class is highly motivated, you will see higher rates of on-task behavior and experience decreased disciplinary problems, fewer referrals, and less absenteeism; you will find you have more lesson time to devote to the "good stuff." Different students must be reached on different levels, but if you are diligent, you will find a way to inspire each of your students. Make sure each student is aware that you are expecting his or her success because you know he or she *can* succeed. Make the same effort to reach each student on more than one level, motivating them externally and intrinsically. Inspire them, and you may just find that they return the favor.

> Students' motivation to engage in any behavior will be related to the degree to which they value the rewards of that behavior and their expectation of succeeding at the behavior.

GENERATE ENTHUSIASM IN YOUR STUDENTS!

Use these strategies, alone or in combination, to increase students' intrinsic motivation.

1. ***Explain how an activity will be useful to students.*** For example, when discussing a historical event, emphasize how it relates to current events in the country or your state.

2. ***Provide a vision of what students will eventually be able to do.*** Each student should know what he will be able to do at the end of the year that he was not able to do at the beginning, if he follows your directions and works hard.

3. ***Relate new tasks to previously learned skills.*** Students should understand how what they have already mastered is useful in understanding new skills. Creating a sense of continuity in learning helps students remember the new information.

4. ***Rally student enthusiasm, especially for challenging tasks.*** Give a pep talk!

IMPLEMENT EFFECTIVE INSTRUCTIONAL PRACTICES

1. ***Use an effective presentational style.*** Students are more likely to pay attention to a teacher who is dynamic, clear, humorous, and excited about her subject than a teacher who is confusing, boring, or talks in a monotone.

2. ***Actively involve students in lessons.*** For example, ask questions, assign tasks for students to work on independently or in pairs, initiate brainstorming sessions, set up role-plays, bring in visual aids, or guide practice of tasks.

3. ***Ensure high rates of student success.*** Students learn faster when they get predominantly correct answers. Provide clear enough instruction and frequent enough practice opportunities to ensure that students will get approximately 90% correct on most tasks.

4. ***Provide students with immediate performance feedback.*** A student who is making mistakes needs to know it as soon as possible in order to learn from those mistakes.

PROVIDE NONCONTINGENT ATTENTION

Take every possible opportunity to provide each student with noncontingent attention. Give students time and attention not because of anything they've done, but just because you notice and value them as people. When they feel noticed and valued, they are more likely to be motivated to engage in appropriate behaviors.

- ✓ Greet your students.
- ✓ Show an interest in students' work.
- ✓ Invite students to ask for assistance.
- ✓ When time permits, have a conversation with a student or a group of students.
- ✓ Make a special effort to greet or talk to any student with whom you've had a recent interaction regarding a misbehavior. This lets the student know that you do not hold a grudge and you are prepared for a fresh start.

GIVE POSITIVE FEEDBACK

Give students positive feedback on their successes in a variety of ways. Positive feedback confirms for students that they are on the right track and increases the probability that they will demonstrate the same behaviors in the future.

Pay particular attention to high-structure classes. The greater the number of high-needs students, the greater the need for you to provide frequent positive feedback.

If a student responds negatively to positive feedback, consider whether the student is embarrassed by the feedback, is trying to maintain a tough image, or does not know how to handle success appropriately. Modify your feedback by making it more private or more succinct and businesslike. You may switch from giving specific descriptive feedback to simply interacting with the student when she is behaving responsibly.

> ## FEEDBACK
>
> Feedback should be . . .
> - Accurate
> - Specific and descriptive
> - Contingent
> - Age appropriate
> - Given in a manner that fits your own style

INTERACT POSITIVELY

Plan to interact at least three times more often with students when they are behaving appropriately than when they are misbehaving. Your interactions with students are considered positive or negative based on the behavior the student is engaged in at the time you attend to him. If a student is off task and you ask him to get back to work, that is a negative interaction—even if your demeanor was pleasant and helpful.

The behavior you pay the most attention to is the behavior you will get more of in the future. That is, if you have more interactions with students when they are behaving appropriately, you will see an increase in positive behavior over time. If you have more interactions with students when they are behaving inappropriately, you will see an increase in negative behavior over time.

> The behavior you pay the most attention to is the behavior you will get more of in the future.

Week of

NOTES

	MONDAY	**TUESDAY**
TIME		

Balance your instructional activities.

WEDNESDAY	THURSDAY	FRIDAY

Make sure you have a balance of activities such as teacher-directed instruction, independent work, and cooperative/peer group tasks • Watch for "too much of a good thing." For example, you may like cooperative groups but inadvertently allot them a disproportionate amount of time in your class period.

Week of

NOTES

TIME

MONDAY	TUESDAY

Teach and re-teach.

WEDNESDAY	THURSDAY	FRIDAY

During independent work periods, students can be prone to misbehavior • Remember to periodically re-teach your expectations and inspire students to manage their own behavior.

NOTES

TIME

MONDAY

TUESDAY

*Take 15 seconds at the end of each period
to help students succeed the next day.*

At least once a week, devote 15 seconds at the end of each period to identify any student who had a rough day—lots of negative interactions • Write their names on a sticky note and place the note in your planner • The note will remind you to increase your positive interactions with those students.

Include • Opportunities to Respond

reference

See *DSC*, pp. 265–267

Student engagement in your lessons is a critical variable in classroom management. Active responding keeps students on task and paying attention, and provides you with feedback on students' understanding of course content. Students who are actively engaged learn more and are less likely to exhibit misbehavior. The Opportunities to Respond Observation Sheet will help you determine the degree to which students are engaged. By taking snapshots of how often a sample of four students responds during instruction, you can determine if you need to modify your instruction.

TO DO

Collect data on student engagement using the Opportunities to Respond Observation Sheet.

WHEN: During the fourth month of school and in mid- to late February.

HOW TO USE THE OPPORTUNITIES TO RESPOND OBSERVATION SHEET

sample

1. Copy the sheet on the next page.
2. Target any classes that are having trouble staying focused or misbehave frequently during lessons.
3. Determine whether you will record video and observe yourself, or whether you will have a colleague observe your lesson. Exchanging observations with a colleague is ideal.
4. Identify four students of different abilities to observe.
5. Record the start and stop time of the lesson. Record a "V" on the observation sheet when the student makes a verbal response and a "W" when the student makes a written response.
6. Determine the average number of responses the students make per minute.
7. Analyze the data. Are Opportunities to Respond high, or do you need to implement new strategies to increase active engagement? Research has shown that learning is maximized when students respond between 4–6 times per minute with 80 percent accuracy on new material, and 9–12 times per minute with 90 to 95 percent accuracy during drill and practice work. (There is little research on optimal response rates for secondary students, but evidence seems to indicate that the more students are actively engaged in the lesson content, the more content they learn.)
8. Repeat with four other students at a later date. Check for increased response rates.

Exhibit F.1

Opportunities to Respond Observation Sheet:
Reproducible Form

Teacher: __Ms. Montoya__

Observer: __Mrs. Nguyen__   Date: __10/4__

Activity: __Pre-Algebra__

Lesson start time: __12:50__   Lesson end time: __1:30__

Duration of Observation (number of minutes): __10__

Student 1	Student 2	Student 3	Student 4
V, V, W, W, V, V, V, V, V, V, W, W, V, V, V, W, V, V, V, V W. V	W, W, W, W, V, V, V, V, V, V, W, W, V, V, V, W, W, V, V, W, W	V, W, W, W, V, V, V, V, W, V, V, V, W, W,	V, V, V, W, W, W, W, V, V, V, W, W, V, V, V, V, V, W, W, V

Mark a V for each verbal response. Mark a W for each written response.

Total number of responses: __76__ divided by 4 equals: __19__
(average number of responses)

Number of minutes divided by average number of responses equals __1.9__
(average responses per minute)

Notes on subjective perception of the degree of student engagement in the lesson:

All but one student seemed attentive during presentation of new material. One student appeared to be reading a different assignment and did not respond to most group questions.

Analysis and Plan of Action

4th Period—Pre-Algebra

Although most students seemed attentive during the lesson, Mr. Montoya wants to increase Opportunities to Respond from the current 1.9 per minute to at least 5 per minute. He will meet with Mrs. Murphy (department head) to brainstorm possible ways to do this.

Exhibit F.1
Opportunities to Respond Observation Sheet:
Reproducible Form

Teacher: _____ Date: _____

Observer: _____

Activity: _____

Lesson start time: _____ Lesson end time: _____

Duration of Observation (number of minutes): _____

Student 1	Student 2	Student 3	Student 4

Mark a V for each verbal response. Mark a W for each written response.

Total number of responses: _____ divided by 4 equals: _____
(average number of responses)

Number of minutes divided by average number of responses equals _____
(average responses per minute)

Notes on subjective perception of the degree of student engagement in the lesson:

Analysis and Plan of Action

NOTES

MONDAY

TUESDAY

TIME

Humor can be a powerful and effective way to respond to misbehavior.

WEDNESDAY	THURSDAY	FRIDAY

A quick humorous comment can sometimes diffuse a tense moment. This must not involve sarcasm or ridicule on the part of the teacher.

Week of

NOTES

TIME

MONDAY

TUESDAY

Interact positively with families throughout the year.

WEDNESDAY	THURSDAY	FRIDAY

You can communicate with families through newsletters, posting class information and assignments to a school website (combined with paper copies), face-to-face contacts, phone calls, notes on homework, and sharing goals • Talk with your colleagues and share best ideas.

NOTES

MONDAY | **TUESDAY**

TIME

Check your class organization.

WEDNESDAY	THURSDAY	FRIDAY

Reflect on student behavior in relationship to your schedule of activities • If there tends to be more frequent misbehavior during particular activities, consider modifying the schedule or adjusting your instructional techniques to keep students more engaged.

Reevaluate • Ratios of Interactions

reference

See *DSC*, pp. 243–250.

A high ratio of teacher attention to responsible behavior vs. misbehavior is essential to a well-run classroom. Earlier, you monitored your students at a particular time of the day. For this activity, you may wish to repeat this activity by monitoring: a) the same time of day, b) a different time of day, c) your attention to a specific misbehavior, or d) a specific student or students who have difficulty.

TO DO

Use the Ratio of Interactions Monitoring Form to determine whether your interactions with your class or a student are primarily positive. Based on this data, increase your positive interactions as needed.

HOW TO USE THE RATIO OF INTERACTIONS MONITORING FORM

1. Make a copy of the Ratio of Interactions Monitoring Form on p. 37.
2. Determine what you will measure—a time period, a particular behavior, or a specific student. Set up a coding system. (See the examples on the next page.)

If . . .	Then monitor ratios of interactions for . . .
During one or more periods of the day, students fail to meet expectations . . .	This time period. • Video or audiotape a 30-minute period. • Use the Ratio of Interactions Monitoring Form on p. 37.
Most students are on task and respectful but have difficulty with a specific behavior such as blurting out or talking with each other . . .	A specific behavior. • Monitor across a day or period (in a middle school). • Carry the Ratio of Interactions Monitoring Form (p. 37) on a clipboard. See Example 1 on the next page, or keep data on a note card kept in your pocket.
Most students are on task and respectful, but a specific student or students has difficulty meeting expectations . . .	A specific student or students. • Monitor across a day or period (in a middle school). • Carry the Ratio of Interactions Monitoring Form (p. 37) on a clipboard. See Example 1 on the next page, or keep data on a note card kept in your pocket.

3. Make sure you understand that positive and negative interactions are based on student behavior. Interactions are positive if student behavior was positive at the time of your interaction. Interactions are negative if student behavior was negative at the time of the interaction—regardless of tone or what you say.
4. Monitor positive and negative interactions and tally them on the form or card.
5. Calculate your ratio of positive to negative interactions. For example:

    10 positive interactions to 20 negative interactions = 1:2

    20 positive interactions to 5 negative interactions = 4:1

6. Analyze your ratio of positive to negative interactions. Did you achieve at least an overall 3:1 ratio of positive to negative interactions?
7. If needed, work on increasing positive interactions and decreasing negative interactions. Watch for improvements in student behavior. Then repeat this activity.

REMINDERS

- Engage in frequent positive and noncontingent interactions. Greet students. Show an interest in their work. Converse with students as time allows.
- Scan the class frequently. Catch students engaging in responsible behavior. Provide descriptive feedback!
- Identify specific times during each period when you will give students positive descriptive feedback on their individual or class performance.
- Identify prompts that will remind you to observe and compliment students on a responsible behavior.
- Each time you interact with a student engaged in negative behavior, tell yourself you owe the student three positive interactions.
- Send positive descriptive notes home, when appropriate.

POSITIVE *Interactions*

If student behavior is appropriate at the time of the interaction, the interaction is positive.

NEGATIVE *Interactions*

If student behavior is inappropriate at the time of the interaction, the interaction is negative.

samples

EXAMPLE 1: SPECIFIC BEHAVIOR

Exhibit B.3
Ratio of Interactions Monitoring Form with a Particular Behavior: Reproducible Form

Teacher: **Mrs. Hazarbedian**   Date: **3/17**

Behavior: **Respecting Others**

Coding System:

M = Male   TI = Teacher-directed lesson   T = Transition (end)
F = Female   I = Independent work

Label the positive and negative behavior that will be monitored (e.g., Attention to Respect & to Disrespect).

Attention to Positive **Respect for Others** (behavior label)	Attention to Negative **Disrespect** (behavior label)
M-TI, F-TI, F-I, F-I, M-I	M-TI, M-TI, F-TI, M-I, F-I

NOTE: Decide if you will post

Analysis and Plan of Act

Analysis and Plan of Action

2nd Period—American History

The ratio of positive to negative interactions related to respecting others is 1:1. Mrs. Hazarbedian will identify more opportunities to pay attention to respectful behavior, especially when she is presenting new material and leading class discussions.

EXAMPLE 2: SPECIFIC STUDENT

Exhibit B.2
Ratio of Interactions Monitoring Form with a Particular Student: Reproducible Form

Teacher: **Mr. Fleming**   Date: **4/15**

Student's Name: **Rasheef**

Coding System:

BC = Before class
TI = Teacher-directed instruction
P = Partners

L = Lining up
G = Discussion group
ED = End of day

Note *every* interaction you have with the student.

Attention to Positive	Attention to Negative
BC, TI, L, L, G, ED	TI, G, G, G, P, P, P, P

Analysis and Plan of Act

Analysis and Plan of Action

6th Period—English

The ratio of Mr. Fleming's positive to negative interactions with Rasheef is 0.75:1 (more negatives to positives). Mr. Fleming will identify more opportunities for positive feedback during discussion groups and partner work, where Rasheef tends to lose focus and become too loud. Mr. Fleming will also seek out opportunities to interact with Rasheef when he is on task during lessons.

Positive interactions are integral to a positive classroom climate.

NOTES

MONDAY	TUESDAY

TIME

Teach students strategies for success.

WEDNESDAY	THURSDAY	FRIDAY

Do your students have a way to manage their homework and independent work? If not, teach students how to manage their work with assignment sheets or to-do lists • Teach students the great satisfaction of checking off completed work.

NOTES

MONDAY | **TUESDAY**

TIME

Teach and re-teach with patience and endurance.

WEDNESDAY	THURSDAY	FRIDAY

If a student has chronic behavioral problems, don't take it personally • Respond calmly to misbehavior but continue to focus on maintaining a high ratio of positive interactions • Work with colleagues to develop a behavior intervention plan and/or study *DSC*, Chapter 9.

NOTES

MONDAY

TUESDAY

TIME

Give students a vision of what they will eventually be able to do.

WEDNESDAY	THURSDAY	FRIDAY

Keep students oriented toward goals • Explain how the materials and skills they are learning now will benefit them in the future • Help them understand how note-taking will help them be successful in high school, in college, and in various occupations.

Week of

TIME	MONDAY	TUESDAY

Keep motivation high!

WEDNESDAY	THURSDAY	FRIDAY

Reinforce responsible behavior with your ongoing positive feedback at the end of instructional activities • Set goals for continued growth and improved behavior.

Correct • Respond Consistently to Student Misbehavior

references

See *DSC*, pp. 89–128 and 203–232.

Your classroom rules communicate to students your expectations about what behavior is acceptable and what is not (see pp. 4–5). Nevertheless, some students will misbehave. When you are sure that students understand your rules, plan to move from informative early-stage corrective techniques to consequences that impose a penalty for breaking a rule. Preplanning your response to misbehavior makes your corrections more effective. This is true for both early-stage misbehavior and more chronic rule violations. By developing and mentally rehearsing the application of corrective consequences to various misbehaviors, you reduce the probability that you will be rattled, frustrated, or upset by student misbehavior.

1. Plan to implement the corrective consequence consistently.
2. Make sure the corrective consequence fits the severity and frequency of the misbehavior.
3. Plan to implement the consequence unemotionally.
4. Plan to interact with the student briefly at the time of the misbehavior without arguing.

Corrective consequences appropriate for secondary classrooms include loss of points, time owed, time-out, restitution, detention, demerits, and—for the most severe misbehaviors—office referral.

Correct • Chronic Misbehavior

For students who continue to misbehave in spite of rules and consequences, individual behavior plans are necessary. Correction procedures can be considered effective only if they reduce the occurrence of the misbehavior they address in the long term. (Don't fall into the Criticism Trap! See p. 36.) Because most chronic misbehavior serves a purpose for the student and because there are many different reasons for misbehavior, correction efforts will be more effective if they address underlying causes of those behaviors.

Implement basic interventions first, moving to more complex interventions only when necessary. Always try the easiest intervention strategies first. See *DSC*, pp. 205–214 for intervention levels and suggested strategies.

Exhibit 9.1
Goal Contract

Student __Todd Ogden__
Class __Physical Science__

Description of problem __Leaves seat to talk with other students; distracts/ disturbs classmates__

Goal __Demonstrate self-control by remaining in your seat and not disturbing others__

Student responsibilities for achieving the goal __Work quietly at your desk. Reduce number of misbehaviors: disturbing others, being out of seat. Use signal—upright book on corner of desk—to let me know you need help with your work (instead of asking other students)__

Teacher support responsibilities __Monitor behavior across the next two weeks. Respond to student's requests for help. Provide positive feedback.__

Evaluation procedures __Misbehavior Recording Sheet will be filled in during the next two weeks. We will then meet to discuss the results. Goal is to have no more than 3 misbehaviors recorded in the second week.__

Date of goal evaluation __5/12__
Student's signature __Todd Ogden__
Teacher's signature __Mrs. Detwiler__

Develop an intervention plan for awareness, ability, attention-seeking, or habitual/purposeful misbehaviors. Continually demonstrate to the student that positive behavior leads to positive results. Have corrective consequences that are appropriate for the problem behavior. See *DSC*, pp. 214–228.

Exhibit 9.1

Goal Contract

Student _____

Class _____

Description of problem _____
_____

Goal _____
_____

Student responsibilities for achieving the goal _____
_____
_____
_____

Teacher support responsibilities _____
_____
_____
_____

Evaluation procedures _____
_____
_____
_____

Date of goal evaluation _____

Student's signature _____

Teacher's signature _____

NOTES

MONDAY | **TUESDAY**

TIME

Arguing with an adolescent is like mud wrestling a pig.
You both get dirty, and the pig loves it!

— *Source unknown*

WEDNESDAY	THURSDAY	FRIDAY

Keep responding to misbehavior calmly and consistently • For every correction, make sure you interact with the student at least three times while the student is behaving responsibly • Remember, misbehavior is an instructional opportunity!

NOTES

MONDAY	TUESDAY

TIME

Teaching is both a science and an art.

WEDNESDAY	THURSDAY	FRIDAY

Part of the teacher's art is theater • Make your lessons fun, entertaining, and interesting • If your lessons are interesting, many behavior problems dissolve away.

NOTES

_____
_____
_____
_____
_____
_____
_____
_____
_____
_____
_____
_____
_____
_____
_____
_____
_____
_____
_____
_____
_____
_____
_____
_____
_____

TIME	MONDAY	TUESDAY

"When you are dog tired at night, could it be that you have been growling all day?"

— *Anonymous*

WEDNESDAY	THURSDAY	FRIDAY

If you feel exhausted and discouraged at the end of the day, you may have fallen into the Criticism Trap • Focus on increasing positive feedback, and you will be tired but excited at the end of the day.

Week of

NOTES

TIME	MONDAY	TUESDAY

Keep preaching your important Guidelines for Success—right up to the last day of class.

WEDNESDAY	THURSDAY	FRIDAY

Plan to "preach" your Guidelines for Success • Preaching involves teaching and inspiring over and over, week after week.

Re-Analyze • Patterns of Misbehavior

reference

See *DSC*, pp. 251–256

Classroom management is an ongoing process that requires perseverance. Over the course of the year, behavior can improve, but it may also periodically deteriorate. As you are nearing the end of the year, it is important to remain vigilant. Do you perceive a great deal of misbehavior? Is misbehavior increasing in your classroom? If the answer is yes, it's the perfect time to use the Misbehavior Recording Sheet to reassess the situation. Data collection will help you to identify:

- ✓ How often the behavior is occurring
- ✓ What misbehavior is occurring
- ✓ Patterns of misbehavior
- ✓ Who is misbehaving
- ✓ Whether you need to intervene

TO DO

Reuse the Misbehavior Recording Sheet on p. 43 of this Planner. Actual data will help you determine whether you need to implement an intervention plan or targeted plans to work with specific types of student misbehavior or specific students.

WHEN: As needed.

HOW TO USE THE MISBEHAVIOR RECORDING SHEET

1. Reproduce the Misbehavior Recording Sheet on p. 43 of this planner. Add student names. See *DSC*, p. 255, for a seating chart version of the form.
2. Put the Misbehavior Recording Sheet on a clipboard so you can keep it with you and record data.
3. Tell students that you will record incidents of misbehavior during the week or day.
4. Use a coding system to record misbehavior whenever you have to correct a student or the group.
5. Analyze the data and determine a plan of action.
   - ✓ Does behavior improve because you are recording data? If yes, repeat this process periodically.
   - ✓ Ask yourself:
     - Is the behavior as disruptive as you thought? If no, no action may be required. If yes, consider re-teaching and/or implementing a classwide motivation system.
     - Can the misbehavior be attributed to one or two individuals? If yes, consider implementing an individual behavior management plan.

Actual data from different times of the year can help you modify your behavioral teaching based on the needs of your students.

In this example , Scott Henry reduced his weekly misbehaviors from eight to two. Todd Ogden increased misbehavior from nine to 12 instances. Rahsaan Thomason reduced his weekly misbehaviors from six to two instances. Overall, the class misbehaviors were at 38 instances in the previous rating. The teacher notes that the class has 20 misbehaviors across the week, with 60% attributed to one student.

The teacher decides that Todd would benefit from an individualized intervention plan to improve and keep his behavior from deteriorating over the last few weeks of school. The teacher decides to overtly work on noncontingent positive interactions with Todd and also sets up a session to do goal contracting. The teacher will work with the student and monitor behavior across the next two weeks. If Todd's behavior improves, the teacher will continue working on positive interactions and goal contracting. If it does not improve, the teacher will study *DSC*, pp. 203–228, and/or consult with the building behavior specialist.

sample

Exhibit C.1
Misbehavior Recording Sheet: Student Name

Date 5/10
Class Period 2   Reminders _____

Name	Mon.	Tues.	Wed.	Thurs.	Fri.	Total
Anderson, Chantel						0
Bahena, Ruben						0
Bell, Justin,						0
Carrouza, Melinda			T			1
Cummings, Teresa						0
Demalski, Lee						1
Diaz, Margo						0
Etienne, Jerry						0
Fujiyama, Kim					5	1
Grover, Matthew						0
Henry, Scott		D	S			2
Isaacson, Chris						0
Kaufman, Jamie						0
King, Mark						0
LaRouche, Janel						0
Morales, Maria Louisa						0
Narlin, Jenny						0
Neely, Jakob						0
Nguyen, Trang						0
Ogden, Todd	TTS	TD	TS	SD	DSD	12
Pallant, Jared						0
Piercey, Dawn	T					1
Reaves, Myra						0
Thomason, Rahsaan		T	0			2
Vandever, Aaron						0
Wong, Charlene						0
Yamamota, James						0

Analysis and Plan of Action

6th Period—Physical Science

Incidents of misbehavior have dropped by almost half since the data collection in November. Todd Ogden now accounts for 60 percent of the misbehavior. The teacher will seek opportunities to increase her positive interactions with the student and will also implement goal contracting for the next two weeks. If the student's behavior does not improve, she will consult the building behavior specialist.

Exhibit 9.1
Goal Contract

Student __Todd Ogden__
Class __Physical Science__

Description of problem __Leaves seat to talk with other students; distracts/__ __disturbs classmates__

Goal __Demonstrate self-control by remaining in your seat and not disturbing__ __others__

Student responsibilities for achieving the goal __Work quietly at your desk.__
__Reduce number of misbehaviors: disturbing others, being out of seat.__
__Use signal—upright book on corner of desk—to let me know you need help__
__with your work (instead of asking other students).__

Teacher support responsibilities _____
__Monitor behavior across the next two weeks.__
__Respond to student's requests for help.__
__Provide positive feedback.__

Evaluation procedures __Misbehavior Recording Sheet will be filled in during the__
__next two weeks. We will then meet to discuss the results. Goal is to have no__
__more than 3 misbehaviors recorded in the second week.__

Date of goal evaluation __5/12__
Student's signature __Todd Ogden__
Teacher's signature __Mrs. Detwiler__

CODE FOR MISBEHAVIOR

O=Off task

H=Hands, feet, and objects used to bother others

T=Talking

D=Disrupting

S=Out of seat

A=Arguing

*Code any other common misbehaviors
you wish to monitor.*

You may wish to compare the example above with the example shown on p. 42—data taken on the same class earlier in the year.

NOTES

MONDAY

TUESDAY

TIME

Teach, analyze, and think ahead.

WEDNESDAY	THURSDAY	FRIDAY

During the final weeks of school, make a list of problem behaviors • It isn't too late to teach new expectations that emphasize the positive opposite of any problem behaviors • Next year, plan to emphasize these expectations at the beginning of the year.

Week of

NOTES

TIME

	MONDAY	TUESDAY

Possess and communicate high expectations for every student's success.

WEDNESDAY	THURSDAY	FRIDAY

Even when you start the year with strong, positive expectations, it can be difficult to sustain them. Try to identify specific negative phrases you may be using, and make an effort to stop. Think of phrases you can use that embrace the positive qualities of your students instead of negative ones.

Week of

MONDAY

TUESDAY

TIME

Rally the enthusiasm of students during the remaining weeks of school.

Be clear about what students are to learn and why • Relate new tasks to previously learned skills • Keep the opportunity to respond high! • Ensure high rates of success with clear instruction and practice.

115

NOTES

MONDAY

TUESDAY

TIME

Keep rates of positive feedback high for those most at risk of failure.

WEDNESDAY	THURSDAY	FRIDAY

Think about it! Research has demonstrated that teachers of students with high rates of behavioral difficulties rarely use praise and often show disapproval rather than approval • This tendency is disheartening in that students who most need positive feedback are least likely to receive it.

Survey and Think Ahead •
Student Satisfaction

reference

See *DSC*, pp. 269–272

The last few weeks of school (and/or after midwinter break next year), use the Student Satisfaction Survey to determine how your students view your classroom program and management plan. This information will help you look ahead to next year—to repeat what went well and to engage in a cycle of continuous improvement with your next class. You may find procedures that can be modified or communicated more clearly to create a stronger program.

The survey can also help you identify aspects of your classroom program that need to be communicated more clearly to students in the future.

TO DO

Use or modify the survey. Use the information gleaned from students to analyze what went well and modify areas that need improvement.

WHEN: During the last few weeks of school or next year after a mid-winter break

HOW TO USE THE STUDENT SATISFACTION SURVEY

1. Check with your administrator to make sure you would not be violating any policies or procedures by giving a survey of this type.
2. Use the example on the next page to develop your own Student Satisfaction Survey. Copy the same questions or develop your own questions to query areas of concern. You may wish to discuss with staff the option of developing a schoolwide survey.
3. When all surveys have been returned, analyze the results. Based on the results, repeat and modify your classroom management plan for next year.

Note: Although survey responses are subjective opinions, the information can help you identify aspects of your classroom that may require further review. For example, if 20 percent of the students say they do not have enough homework, 50 percent say it's just right, and 30 percent say there's too much homework, it's probably just about right.

An Opportunity for Continuous Improvement
Plan ahead. Celebrate and repeat what has gone well.
Then look for patterns of information that will help you fine-tune your classroom management plan for next year.

Exhibit G.1
Student Satisfaction Survey: Reproducible Form

Dear Students,

As we approach this point in the school year, I want to thank you all for your help and support. As a professional trying to meet the needs of all students, I am always looking for ways to improve. You can help by giving me feedback about the strengths and weaknesses you see in my program. Please take a few minutes to fill out the following survey.

Note there is no place to put your name. I will not know who wrote what unless you wish to sign your name. Once you complete the survey, fold it in half and place it in the box by the door.

Sincerely,

Mr. Lincoln

Homework

1. The amount of homework assigned has been:

   ○ Way too much   ✗ A bit too much   ○ About right   ○ Not enough

2. The difficulty of homework has been:

   ○ Way too hard   ○ A bit too hard   ✗ About right   ○ Too easy

Assignments and Class Work

1. The amount of in-class work assigned has been:

   ○ Way too much   ○ A bit too much   ✗ About right   ○ Not enough

2. The difficulty of in-class work has been:

   ○ Way too hard   ○ A bit too hard   ✗ About right   ○ Too easy

3. Most of the time I felt that the work has been:

   ○ Stupid   ○ Boring   ✗ Okay   ○ Interesting   ○ Fun

4. Describe one valuable thing you learned this year: _____

Student Satisfaction Survey: Reproducible Form
(continued)

5. Identify one type of activity there should be more of:

   ○ Lecture   ○ Discussion   ○ Cooperative groups   ✗ Independent work   ○ Simulations

6. Identify one type of activity there should be less of:

   ○ Lecture   ○ Discussion   ✗ Cooperative groups   ○ Independent work   ○ Simulations

Classroom Atmosphere

1. Most of the time, I have . . .

   ○ hated coming to this class   ✗ felt that this class is okay   ○ looked forward to class

Please explain your answer: I really like this class, but I don't like working in cooperative groups.
_____

2. I think the teacher has treated me with respect . . .

   ○ not often   ○ most of the time   ✗ all of the time

Please explain your answer: _____

3. What might I have done differently to make this year a more pleasant and productive experience for you? I think you should ask your students if they want to work in cooperative groups.

   I know there are a lot of us who would rather work independently.
_____

---

notes .....

NOTES

TIME	MONDAY	TUESDAY

Use data to help students stay engaged and successful throughout the last weeks of school.

WEDNESDAY	THURSDAY	FRIDAY

Select and repeat an activity that yielded the most useful information—ACHIEVE Versus Daily Reality Rating Scale (p. 31), Ratio of Interactions Monitoring Form (p. 37), Misbehavior Recording Sheet (p. 43), On-Task Behavior Observation Sheet (p. 57), Opportunities to Respond (p. 81), or Goal Contracting (p. 99).

NOTES

TIME	**MONDAY**	**TUESDAY**

Teaching is a profession.

WEDNESDAY	THURSDAY	FRIDAY

Professionalism requires keeping up to date and a willingness to look at your own behavior with a critical eye • Congratulations! By working through this planner, you have engaged in continuous improvement and your own professional development.

Week of

NOTES

TIME

Your chosen profession is a noble endeavor.

DSC Teacher Planner

"A teacher affects eternity. He can never tell where his influence stops."
—Henry Adams

Teacher Planner Sample

SETTING UP PLANNER PAGES

1. Using your school calendar, enter dates for each week. (Forty-two Weekly Planners are included.)
2. Fill in holidays, vacations, teacher workdays, parent conferences, testing, assembly schedules, etc.
3. Set up a planner schedule.
4. There are 35 writing lines on each weekly planner spread. Divide 35 lines by the number of periods and your lunch period. Use a pencil to draw lines across the planner to separate the periods. Repeat with a pencil or pen in subsequent weeks.
5. Add activities as appropriate for your lessons.

Week of Oct. 19–23

NOTES

You may wish to:

- Keep track of student absences and tardies.
- Note when you need to teach expectations for special events.
- Write reminders to yourself so opportunities to make positive connections with students don't slip by.

Weekly tips provide timely reminders of effective classroom management procedures.

TIME	MONDAY	TUESDAY	WEDNESDAY	THURSDAY
			Contract hour starts–6:50am	Contract hour starts–6:50am
7:00	Contract hour starts–6:50am	Contract hour starts–6:50am	English	History
7:25–8:45 1st period	English	History		
			English	History
8:50– 10:10 2nd period	English	History		
			Lunch	Lunch
10:15–	Lunch	Lunch	Advisory	Advisory
	Advisory	Advisory		
			English	History
	English	History		
period				
			Planning	Planning
	Planning	Planning		
period				
		Anime Club Advisor 2:15–3:30	Staff meeting	
–4:00 School tract 2:45)				

Teach students strategies for success.

Do your students have a way to manage their home[w...] students how to manage their work with assignment sheet[...] great satisfaction of checking off completed work.